Zip, Zap, Blip

by Jennifer Gonzalez
illustrated by Jason Dove

Practice Decodable 28

I0806511

Mc Graw Hill Education

Bothell, WA • Chicago, IL • Columbus, OH • New York, NY

MHEonline.com

Send all inquiries to:
McGraw-Hill Education
8787 Orion Place
Columbus, OH 43240

ISBN: 978-0-02-136255-4
MHID: 0-02-136255-6

Printed in China

8 9 10 11 12 DSS 27 26 25 24 23

Jets Zip And Zap

Zip! Fran makes her jet zip!
She has fun!

Zap! Mom makes her jet zap!
She has fun!

Mom jumps up!
"Yes!" said Fran.

The Game Ends

Jake the cat did not like jet games.

There is a plug.

There is Jake.

Did Jake stop the jet game?

Snap! Zap! Blip!

Jake did stop it.

Yet they had fun, said Mom.